Frogs

Don McLeese

Rourke
Educational Media
rourkeeducationalmedia.com

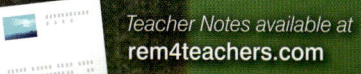

Teacher Notes available at
rem4teachers.com

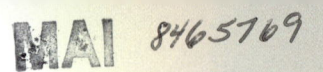

© 2013 Rourke Educational Media

All rights reserved. No part of this book may be reproduced or utilized in any form or by any means, electronic or mechanical including photocopying, recording, or by any information storage and retrieval system without permission in writing from the publisher.

www.rourkeeducationalmedia.com

PHOTO CREDITS: Cover: ©; Title Page: © Mark Kostich; 2: © Robert Daveant; Page 4: © Djtaylor, Alasdair Thomson, Djtaylor, Jolanta Dabrowska; ©; Page 5: © Lee Pettet, Holly Goober, Daniela Agius, Isselee, Ryan Sartoski; Page 6: © Shaun Lowe; Page 7: © Rosemarie Gearhart; Page 8: © Alexey Lisovoy, Mustafanc; Page 9: © Pavel Kratochvil, Pierre Chouinard, dirk ercken, Karen Troup; Page 10: © Eric Isselée, 4x6, Justin Horrocks, Paul Tessier; Page 11: © Paul Tessier; Page 12: © Mark Kostich, Photowitch; Page 13: © David Anderson, Alasdair Thomson; Page 14: © Linda Hides, humbak; Page 15: © Paula Mozdrzewska, Paulina Lenting-Smulders, CountryStyle Photography; Page 16: © wikipedia, stock_art; Page 17: © Jodi Matthews; Page 18: © David Persson, Servet Gürbüz; Page 19: © macropixel, pop_jop; Page 20: © Phil Augustavo, Ethan Finkelstein, Barun Patro; Page 21: © Michał Rózewski ; Page 22: © Donald Bowers;

Edited by Precious McKenzie

Cover Design by Renee Brady
Interior Design by Cory Davis

Library of Congress PCN Data

Frogs / Don McLeese
(Eye to Eye with Animals)
ISBN 978-1-61810-113-6 (hard cover) (alk. paper)
ISBN 978-1-61810-246-1 (soft cover)
Library of Congress Control Number: 2011944396

Rourke Educational Media
Printed in the United States of America,
North Mankato, Minnesota

Rourke
Educational Media

rourkeeducationalmedia.com

customerservice@rourkeeducationalmedia.com • PO Box 643328 Vero Beach, Florida 32964

Table of Contents

Double Lives 4

The World of Frogs 8

Frogs and Toads 12

Hopping Around the World 16

Frogs, Toads, and People 20

Glossary 23

Index 24

Chapter 1
Double Lives

Have you ever imagined what it would be like to lead a double life? If you were a frog you could!

Frogs are members of the animal group classified as **amphibians**. The word amphibian originally meant *double life*. In fact, almost 90 percent of amphibians are some kind of frog or toad. Frogs begin their lives as water animals. This is where the female frog lays her eggs. Once the eggs hatch, out comes the **tadpoles**.

Eggs

Adult Frog

Embryo

Tadpole

Some tadpoles are so small they are hard to see, although others may be six or seven inches (13-18 centimeters) long. Tadpoles live in the water, and they have long tails to help them swim. They eat plants, but some of them eat frog eggs or even other tadpoles!

It takes about 12 to 16 weeks for a tadpole to become a frog. A number of things change during that time. It grows legs. It develops **lungs** which allow it to breathe on land. It develops a new **digestive system** which allows it to eat insects, worms, and small animals. Eventually, it loses its tail.

Tadpole

Tadpole Frog

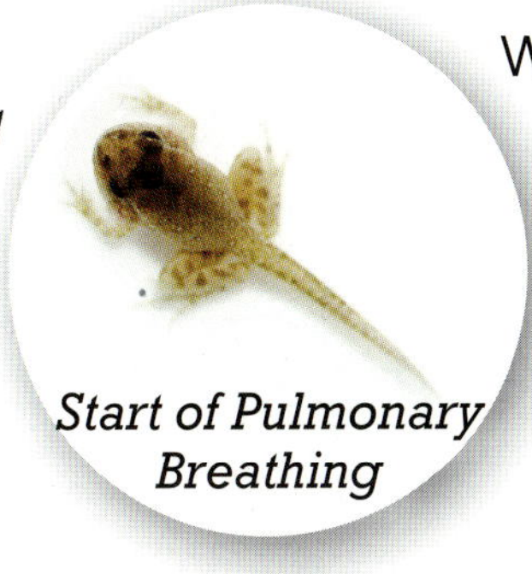

Start of Pulmonary Breathing

Legs Break Through

Tadpole

Most frogs begin their lives as water animals but then become land animals. They look very different as frogs than they did as tadpoles. On their own, they generally live six to eight years. Many of them die when they are eaten by bigger, stronger animals.

Frogs that are pets can live twice as long as frogs in the wild because there aren't predators around to eat them.

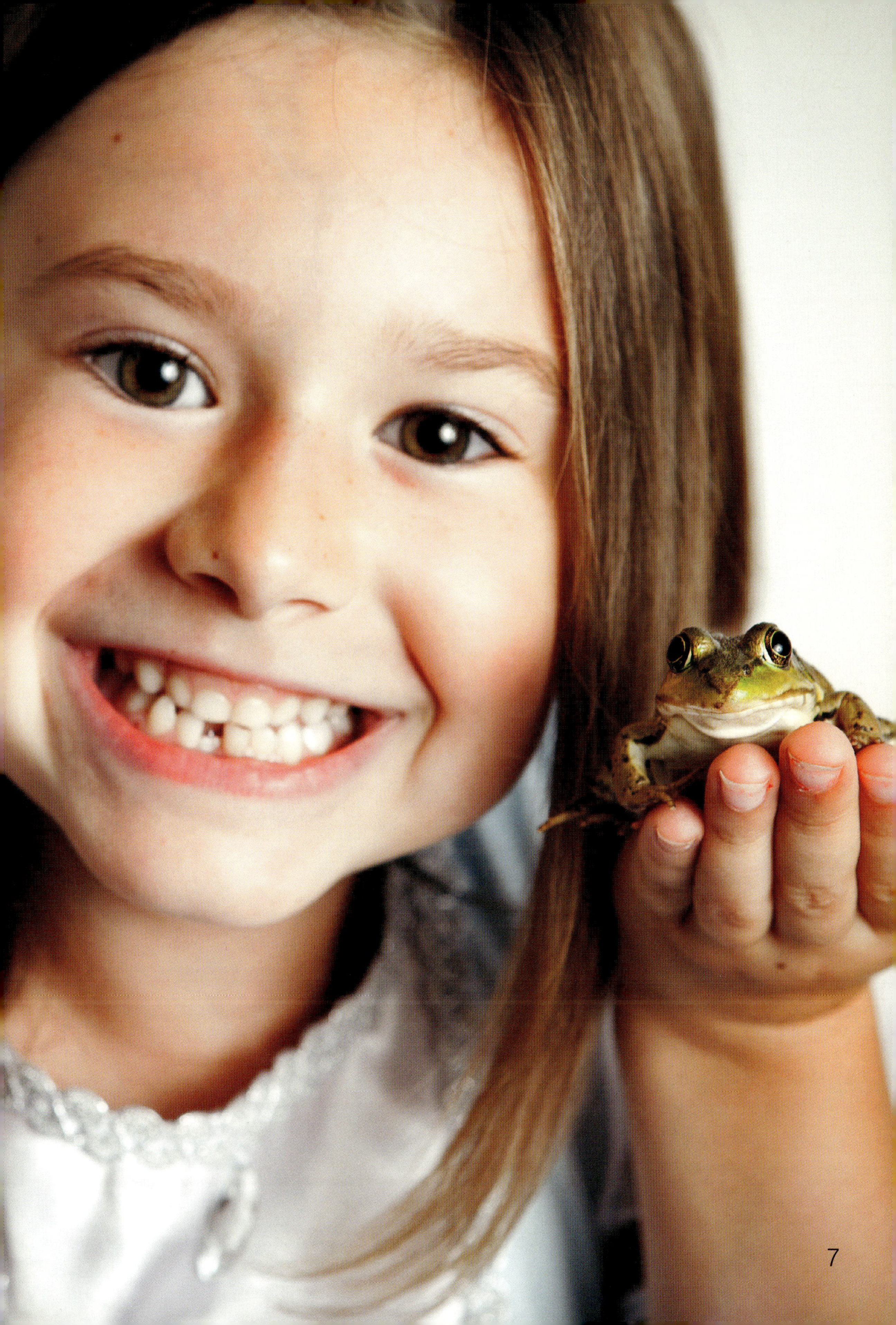

Chapter 2

The World of Frogs

Frogs are found practically everywhere in the world, except in places like Antarctica where it is very cold. Most move from water to land as they develop from tadpoles into frogs. Some kinds, or **species**, of frogs live their entire lives in the water, or very near it. Others climb trees and live there. Others live underground. They dig holes and **burrow** their way under the grass to hibernate.

Ground Frog

FUN FACT

The wood frog can live with 65% of its body frozen. Scientists discovered that its glucose centers around its vital organs, protecting organs even though the rest of its body could be frozen solid.

Wood Frog

Brown Frog

Poison Dart Frog

Red-eyed Tree Frog

American Bull Frog

Scientists believe that frogs have been around for 180 million years! Over that time, frogs have developed into almost 5,000 different species. Every species is a little different, but most frogs have a lot of things in common.

Frogs typically have short bodies and no tails. The tail disappears after the tadpole stage. Their feet are **webbed**. Most of them are green or brown, or some combination of the colors, to blend in with the ground, grass, and trees in areas where they live. Others have bright colors and patterns.

Frogs, and all amphibians, are **cold-blooded**. This means that the temperature of their body is the same as the temperature of the air or water around them. People are **warm-blooded** with a body temperature that stays the same inside, no matter how hot or cold it is.

Frog Body Temperature
82 Degrees F
(28 Degrees Celsius)

Human Body Temperature
98.6 Degrees F
(37 Degrees Celsius)

Water Temperature 82 Degrees F

Frogs are very good jumpers, with strong legs. And, they have big eyes that stick out from the front and sides of their head. Their bulging eyes let them see in almost all directions.

◀◀ *Their good eyesight helps them find food and avoid other animals that like to eat frogs!*

Did You Know?

Scientists think frogs were the very first land animals with vocal cords. Guess what? Only the male frogs make sounds.

Spring Peeper Frog

10

Most frogs eat other animals, insects, and worms rather than plants which means that they are **carnivores**. The frog has a very sticky tongue, which it uses to capture insects and other forms of food. Their voices make a call which is called a **croak**, sounding like "RIB-bit" in a raspy, lower tone. Some frogs make sounds like a chirp.

Among the frogs that live in the United States, the largest is the **bullfrog**. It can be eight inches (20 centimeters) long. Bullfrogs are great jumpers. They can jump as far as six feet (1.8 meters)! And, bullfrogs eat practically anything they can swallow, including insects, fish, turtles, and other frogs.

Big Eyes

Strong Legs

Short Body

Webbed Feet

Chapter 3
Frogs and Toads

Many people get confused about the differences between frogs and **toads**. Toads are a type of frog. But, they have differences. Most frogs have a smoother body that some people call **slimy**, and they are skinnier than toads. They also have bigger eyes. Frogs are better jumpers, and they usually live near the water.

Red-eyed Tree Frog

Toads have rougher, bumpier skin, a wider body, and they don't need to live near water. They run or hop rather than take big jumps. Toads have a different cartilage system in their bodies than frogs. Even the way they lay eggs is different. Many toads lay eggs in a long chain or even give birth to live young!

Common Toad

Differences Between Toads and Frogs

Large Ridge & Big Eyes

Chubby Body

Bumpy Skin

Common Toad

Short Legs

Bulging Eyes

Smooth or Slimy Skin

Teeth

Strong, Long Legs

Long, Webbed Feet

Tree Frog

Toads and Their Lifestyles

Young Toads

Toads Laying Eggs

Toads Living on Land

Chapter 4
Hopping Around the World

Scientists continue to find new frogs all around the world. On the island of New Guinea, there is a recently discovered frog that is smaller than a dime. Not only is this the smallest frog in the world, it is the smallest animal with four legs. There are plenty of other interesting frogs throughout the world.

Discovered in New Guinea, Paedophryne amauensis is believed to be the smallest frog in the world.

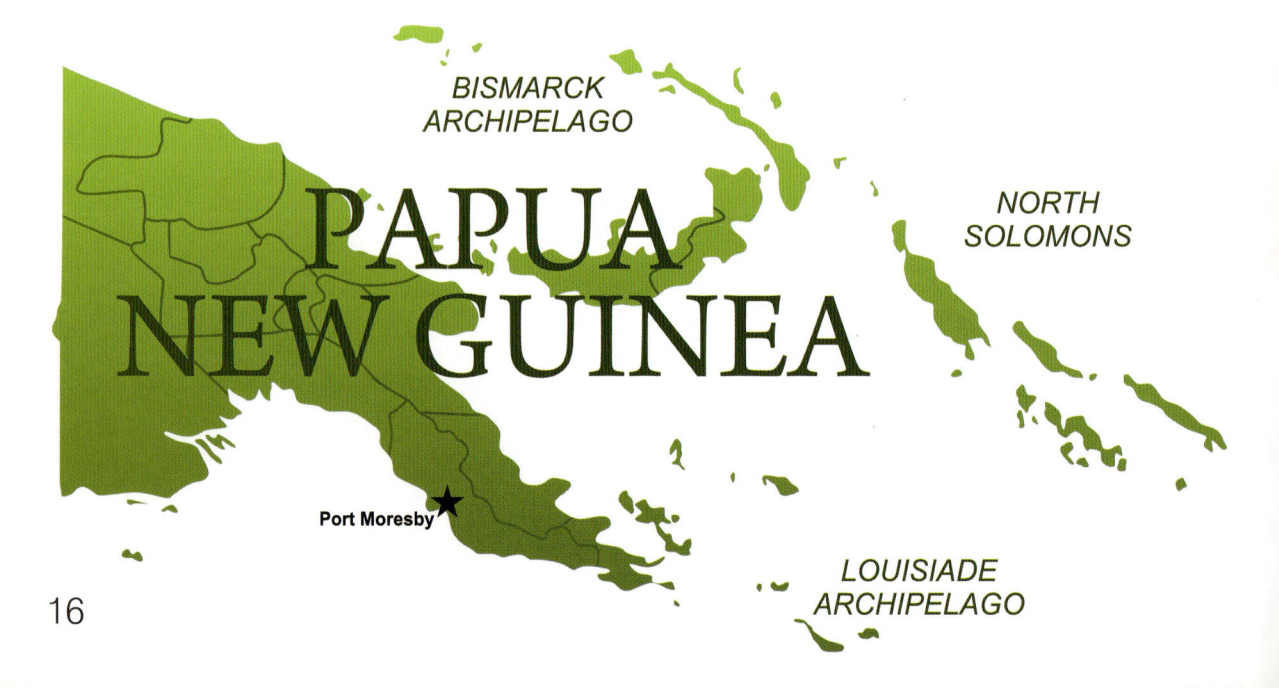

Scientists study frogs, both alive and dead, to learn about pollution and climate changes.

17

There are plenty of other interesting frogs throughout the world. The Amazon Horned Frog, found in South America along the Amazon River, is big and fat! They can weigh as much as one pound (454 grams)! They hide under leaves so that only their head shows, and they capture other animals with their sharp teeth. They have a very big appetite and love to eat!

Amazon Horned Frog

South America

Amazon River

Brazil

★ **Brasília**

Wallace's Flying Frogs can be found in the trees of the jungles of Borneo and Malaysia. Do they really fly? They seem to as they leap as far as 50 feet (15 m) down from the trees to eat or mate. Because of the way they float through the air, they are sometimes called parachute frogs.

Wallace's Flying Frog

Chapter 5
Frogs, Toads, and People

As with so many animals, the biggest danger to frogs is people. Water **pollution** by people can poison the places where frogs lay their eggs and where tadpoles develop.

When towns and cities grow, concrete and steel often take the place of the forests and marshes where frogs live. Overdevelopment causes habitat destruction for frogs.

Red-eyed Tree Frog

Scientists use frogs in medical experiments to test new drugs. And, some people like eating frogs, frog legs in particular.

We wouldn't want frogs to disappear. They are one of nature's best pest controllers. Frogs eat insects which would otherwise bother people and destroy the plants that people use for food.

Frogs have been around for a long time. We want to make sure they continue to exist a lot longer!

How You Can Help Save Frogs:

1. Use nontoxic household cleansers.
2. Use fewer pesticides in your garden or pond.
3. Get involved with amphibian conservation organizations.

Glossary

amphibians (am-FIB-ee-uhns): species of cold-blooded animals that live in the water when young, then develop lungs and live on land as an adult

bullfrog (BULL-frawg): one of the largest frogs with one of the lowest, deepest voices

burrow (BUR-oh): to dig a hole or a tunnel and live in it

carnivores (KAHR-nuh-vorz): animals that eat other animals; meat eaters

cold-blooded (KOHLD BLUHD-id): a body temperature that changes according to the temperature of the air or water outside the body

croak (KROHK): to make a deep, hoarse, or raspy sound with the voice

digestive system (dye-JES-tihv SIS-tuhm): the body's process of breaking down food and taking from it what it needs

lungs (LUHNGS): organs inside the chest that fill with air like a bag and let an animal breathe

pollution (puh-LOOH-shuhn): waste products, chemicals, or other material that can hurt or poison the water, air, or soil

slimy (SLY-me): moist and slippery

species (SPEE-sheez): a group of animals that are similar

tadpole (TAD-pole): a young frog that lives in the water and has a tail but no legs

toads (TOHDS): amphibians that look like frogs but have rougher skin and don't need to live near water

warm-blooded (WORM BLUHD-id): a body temperature that doesn't change even if it gets hotter or colder outside the body

webbed (WEHBD): having skin or tissue that connects the toes, instead of space between them

Index

Amazon Horned Frog   18
amphibians   4
bullfrog   11
burrow   8
carnivores   11
cold-blooded   10
croak   11
digestive system   5
eggs   4, 13, 15, 20
lungs   5
pollution   20
species   8, 9
tadpole(s)   4, 5, 6, 9, 20
toad(s)   12, 13, 14, 15
Wallace's Flying Frog   19
warm-blooded   10
webbed   9, 11, 14

Websites To Visit

www.kidzone.ws/lw/frogs/

allaboutfrogs.org/

www.kiddyhouse.com/Themes/frogs/

About the Author

Don McLeese is a journalism professor at the University of Iowa. He has written many articles for newspapers and magazines and many books for young students as well.

Ask The Author!
www.rem4students.com